Peer Review

A Short Guide

Jo VanEvery, PhD

Peer Review

Short Guides, vol 4

Copyright © 2019 Jo VanEvery

All rights reserved.

ISBN: 978-1-912040-66-7 (pb) 978-1-912040-65-0 (e-book)

No part of this publication may be reproduced, stored in a retrieval system, or transmitted in any form or by any means, electronic, mechanical, photocopying, recording, or otherwise, without the prior written permission of the copyright owner.

This book is sold subject to the condition that it shall not, by way of trade or otherwise, be lent, resold, hired out, or otherwise circulated without the publisher's prior consent in any form of binding or cover other than that in which it is published and without a similar condition including this condition being imposed on the subsequent purchaser. Under no circumstances may any part of this book be photocopied for resale.

Cover Design: Amy Crook

JO VAN EVERY

Table of Contents

About the Short Guides series 1

About this guide 4

What is peer review? 6

Receiving comments as an author 18

Giving feedback constructively as a reviewer 38

Conclusion: Peer review supports the advancement
of knowledge 63

Notes and further reading 64

Acknowledgements 75

About the author 77

Jo Van Every

About the Short Guides Series

My journey to becoming an academic career guide, though I didn't call it that at the time, began in 2005. In the early years, my work focused on supporting Canadian social science and humanities academics with grant applications. Drawing on my experience as a programme officer and policy analyst at the Social Sciences and Humanities Research Council of Canada, and my own eight-year academic career as a sociologist in the UK, I focused on helping academics understand how funding competitions worked, improving their project descriptions, and advising them on their applications.

Two issues came up repeatedly. The first was the quantity and quality of previous publications. Many of my clients expressed frustration with the publication record required to be competitive, especially if they worked in institutions with heavier teaching loads. The second, related issue was the concept of "impact on the advancement of knowledge." Many academics were confused about why some scholarly publications were more highly valued than others, and how such publications related to the increasingly pressing demand to reach audiences beyond the academy. This confusion had consequences for their ability to frame their research in relation to its likely impact on the advancement of knowledge, as well as their confidence in the importance of the questions they most wanted to research.

The impossibility of addressing these difficulties on a short-term basis (difficulties that, after all, affect much more than just the ability to secure funding) was frustrating for everyone. In 2009, I started shifting my focus to take a longer-term view, creating a website (JoVanEvery.ca) and starting to blog. In 2011, I started A Meeting With Your Writing, a synchronous virtual writing group, as a way of providing practical support to academics who were struggling to protect their writing time due to the pressures of all their other responsibilities. I gradually built a coaching practice that wasn't focused directly on grant applications, sharing what I was learning through my blog.

By 2015, I had over 400 blog posts, most of them still relevant but a bit difficult to find in the archive. The *Short Guides* series organizes, summarizes, and builds on those blog posts to create practical resources based on what I've learned over the years. An important underlying principle of the *Short Guides* is that there are many different ways to do most things. You have particular values and goals. Your brain and body work in particular ways. You work in a specific kind of institution with its own values and goals. Things that used to work well for you stop working. Your priorities change over time. You need to make decisions – and maybe experiment with new strategies – in light of how all these things come together, right now, for you.

Each *Short Guide* focuses on one area of your academic life, providing advice in a format you can apply to your own specific circumstances. I've started with topics related to scholarly writing. They are short, so you can spend more time writing and less time reading about writing or time management. They are practical, suggesting strategies you can try right now. The tone is deliberately conversational. Notes and further reading are at the back, sorted by chapter. I expect you will read each *Short Guide* through from beginning to end when you first acquire it. However, they are really intended to be kept close by, so you can refer to the section that addresses your current frustration as and when needed. Coffee rings have been pre-applied, so don't feel guilty about using a *Short Guide* as a coaster.

Enjoy your writing!

Other Short Guides

- *The Scholarly Writing Process: A Short Guide* (2016)
  ISBN 978-1-912040-64-3 (pb) 978-1-912040-72-8 (eBook)
- *Finding Time For Your Scholarly Writing: A Short Guide* (2018)
  ISBN 978-1-912040-70-4 (pb) 978-1-912040-69-8 (eBook)
- *Scholarly Publishing: A Short Guide* (2019)
  ISBN 978-1-912040-68-1 (pb) 978-1-912040-67-4 (eBook)

About This Guide

This *Short Guide* aims to help scholars engage with the peer-review process, as both reviewers and authors, to contribute meaningfully and confidently to the advancement of knowledge in their fields. Although the role of peers in the evaluation of scholars for funding, hiring, promotion, etc. is also often called "peer review," in this volume I discuss only peer review in the scholarly publishing process. I have also limited the discussion to the roles of authors and reviewers. Although journal editors, and editorial boards, are also comprised of peers, their roles are not discussed in detail in this volume.

Scholars highly value peer review; despite all its shortcomings, peer review is how they collectively shape the boundaries of disciplines and fields of study, and agree on standards of rigour. A core principle of academic freedom is that only your scholarly peers can really judge the quality of your work. Done well, peer review provides substantive editing with the goal of improving the quality of your contribution to knowledge, even when reviewers recommend that a manuscript be rejected. This *Short Guide* complements advice on the ethics of peer review, the specific guidelines provided by journals and presses, and the more general debate about anonymity and openness in peer review.

My objective is to help you to understand the general principles underpinning peer review and to engage in peer review as an author and a reviewer in ways that emphasize the tradition's best elements and minimize its worst abuses. I expect you to refer to sections when you receive a review, or a manuscript to review, for reassurance that you can do this and a quick reminder of basic principles and practical strategies. Like my other *Short Guides*, it is deliberately very short because I know you have enough things on your to-read list. I hope it's helpful.

Jo VanEvery
High Peak, UK

What is Peer Review?

In their short history of the use of peer review in academic publishing, Aileen Fyfe and her colleagues note that it originated in the 18th and 19th centuries, when:

> most scholarly research journals and some academic books were sponsored by learned societies (and later university presses). For such organisations, referring papers to suitably-qualified members of the society or university for close scrutiny before publication was part of an editorial system that was intended to emphasise collective rather than individual responsibility, as well as to decide on the appropriate use of institutional resources.

When they entered the scholarly publishing market in the mid-20th century, commercial publishers then adopted these processes – as did university presses later on – as a means of indicating their commitment to the project of advancing scholarly knowledge. At the same time, peer review spread from the natural sciences to become common in all disciplines.

As I elaborated in *Scholarly Publishing (A Short Guide)*, the primary role of scholarly publishing is to facilitate a formal conversation (sometimes called "debate") among scholars, with the goal of advancing scholarly knowledge. These formal conversations are crucial to the creation of research knowledge. The core values of scholarly communities include both the creation of knowledge as a collective activity and freedom from commercial or political influence in the creation of knowledge. The involvement of commercial presses in publishing, and changes in the relationship between scholarly communities and universities, have heightened the tensions between, on the one hand, academic ideals of openness and the free exchange of ideas to advance knowledge; and, on the other, commercial ideals of secrecy and competitive advantage. Peer review embodies both of these core values, first by inviting peers to inform the decisions made by editors or editorial boards (who are also usually peers) about whether to publish a particular manuscript, and second by inviting peers to provide editorial feedback on manuscripts to ensure the final published version is the best contribution it can be. Peer review thus collectively shapes the scholarly conversation as a whole (which may be considered a field, discipline, or interdisciplinary area) as it makes recommendations about individual contributions to the conversation.

Peer review as gatekeeping

Scholarly conversations are curated in journals and book series, which are also in conversation with each other, collectively forming fields, disciplines, and interdisciplinary areas that may also be institutionalized as scholarly associations and university departments.

Typically, decisions about what is published are made by a journal editor, an acquisitions or series editor of a press, or an editorial board. These decisions will be informed by the comments of peer reviewers with expertise in one or more area relevant to the specific contributions. Collectively, decisions made by reviewers and editors shape the scholarly conversation and the contribution of this particular journal or press to wider conversations in the field, discipline, or interdisciplinary area. Decisions about whether a particular manuscript meets agreed standards of rigour cumulatively define the standards of rigour expected of research in your field and discipline. Maintaining academic control over the conversation (and acceptable questions and approaches within it) and standards of rigour safeguards academic freedom as freedom from commercial and political influence, within the bounds of epistemological possibility.

The decision-making function of peer review is often referred to as "gatekeeping," which can suggest that the boundaries of the conversation are fairly solid (like a wall or fence), with a limited number of clear entry points guarded by some kind of sentry or warden. Gatekeeping suggests the peer reviewer is the sentry opening the gate for the author, refusing the author entry, or sending the author away with clear instructions about what is required to have the gate opened. It can overstate the power of each individual reviewer to permit or deny entry. The work of reviewing manuscripts involves multiple reviewers, an editor, and perhaps an editorial board, precisely because no single individual should have this much power to shape the conversation to their own whims.

Furthermore, the boundaries of a scholarly conversation – in terms of the questions and debates proper to it, standards of rigour, and how one might meet them – are nowhere near as solid as a stone wall. One might consider them more of a fence or flexible barrier, which can be moved, expanded, and contracted. Even if the boundaries are wall-like, the work of authors, reviewers, and editors is the collective work of building and maintaining that wall. This work occasionally involves the destruction of previously solid parts of the wall to allow them to be rebuilt or replaced (what Kuhnians might call "paradigm shifting"), but is usually not quite so drastic.

Peer review may tend towards conserving the existing boundaries of the conversation, adjudicating whether a particular manuscript adds something to the field as currently constructed. However, peer reviewers are also required to recognize the ways in which a particular manuscript could open up a crack in the conversation that would enable creative destruction in the service of the advancement of knowledge and this particular scholarly conversation. Peer reviewers try to distinguish that sort of creative crack from less-welcome forms of destruction, and advise editors accordingly. The boundaries of your field are built collectively and asynchronously.

Peer review as editorial labour

The power inherent in the gatekeeping function of peer review is kept in check, not only by the use of multiple reviewers and the separation of the review from the final decision but also by a strong commitment to constructive criticism to assist the author in meeting the standards of inclusion in the conversation. When you think about it, all published writing is a collaboration, even writing attributed to a single author.

Peer review is part of that collaborative process. In addition to providing expert advice on whether your manuscript will make a significant contribution, reviewers provide editorial comments – usually of the developmental or substantive type, though they may also offer more detailed line edits. The editor may supplement these comments with additional guidance to assist you in making choices where reviewers disagree. In the case of book publishing, the series editor or acquisitions editor may be willing to provide considerable support as you respond to reviewers' comments and revise your proposal or manuscript prior to a contract being issued.

The work peer reviewers do in academic publishing is similar to work done by various kinds of professionals for other writers. For example, writers of fiction and trade non-fiction who publish traditionally will send work that has already gone through several revisions, perhaps with the assistance of a professional editor, to their agent, who will comment on the main ideas, the overall structure, and other big-picture issues as the author refines a draft. When the agent is satisfied that there is a publishable work, they will shop it around to various publishers to secure the best publishing deal for this author. Then the acquisitions editor from the press will read and comment on the manuscript, offering suggestions for improvement. After the revised manuscript is submitted, a copyeditor will offer comments on the details of style, vocabulary, and so on. The author will make further revisions. The final manuscript will be proofread for any remaining errors prior to publication.

In academic publishing, many stages of this work are done by other academics on a volunteer basis. Although peer review involves various types of editing, most academics have not been formally trained in editing and may not even be familiar with standard terms of the profession – such as developmental editing, substantive editing, line editing, copy-editing, and proofreading – nor the different types of work these terms denote. Some journals and presses give detailed guidance to reviewers to mitigate this and direct their comments. However, a lack of formal acknowledgement of, and training in, the skills involved may account for the considerable variability in the nature and tone of reviewers' comments.

The work of those not credited with authorship, who nevertheless were instrumental in the production of the published work, is often formally acknowledged in the front- or backmatter of a book, or in a footnote to a journal article, under the heading "Acknowledgements." The contributions of anonymous peer reviewers are frequently recognized in this way. These acknowledgements make visible labour that might otherwise be invisible.

Peer review and the value of voluntary labour

The tensions between academic ideals of openness and the free exchange of ideas to advance knowledge and commercial ideals of secrecy and competitive advantage affect the ways in which peer review works in contemporary academic environments, where commercial logics are increasingly influential – not only in publishing but also in institutional rankings and government education policy. One of the contentious issues is the voluntary nature of the editorial work done by journal editors, series editors, and peer reviewers.

Academic values of freedom from commercial influence have held relatively strong, despite the increasingly large role commercial publishers play in scholarly publishing. Although there is a lot of resentment about commercial publishers' exploitation of voluntary labour for profit, this has not resulted in large-scale demands for the labour to be remunerated; rather, the profits of those publishers have been questioned, along with their influence on higher-education policy. There have been strong demands for journal and academic book prices to be reduced, alongside a movement for open access, especially where the research was publicly funded. The open-access publishing movement has also created new not-for-profit publishing ventures.

The voluntary nature of peer review also creates workload tensions. Many academics consider their salary to cover the wide range of work they do as scholars, including peer review. An increasingly casualized academic labour market and increasing workloads create the conditions in which the value of this voluntary labour is questioned. Even for those scholars who have relatively secure academic employment, the voluntary labour of peer review is often poorly recognized, either in workload allocation models or in hiring and promotion criteria. This makes sense when you consider that the work only benefits the institution that employs you indirectly, at best.

Your peer-review labour primarily benefits other scholars like yourself. This is why it's called *peer* review. You benefit personally from the peer-review labour of other scholars in these networks. The primary way that you are rewarded for your labour is through diffuse reciprocity. The reciprocity is diffuse in terms of both the connections between you and others in the network and how this labour is distributed over time. The voluntary labour you provide through peer review contributes to the collective advancement of knowledge in a field you are simultaneously collectively defining. There will be times in your career when you have little to contribute and are mainly a recipient of peer-review labour. At other times, you will face considerable demands for this type of labour, and those demands will expand to include membership of editorial boards, editorships, and so on. Although some of these roles have prestige value, seeing the value of this labour in terms of its contribution to knowledge helps you give it appropriate priority and ensures you undertake this work compassionately and ethically.

In addition to these collective benefits, participating in peer review can contribute to your own professional development. As a reviewer, you see work at an earlier stage of development than you might otherwise, which can help you refine your own judgements about the readiness of your writing for submission. Reviewing resubmitted manuscripts gives you insight into how other authors respond to comments. If other reviews of the same paper are shared with all reviewers, you benefit from seeing the range of reviewer comments and styles, as well as editors' comments. As a reviewer, you are also seeing the current work in your field at an early stage. Reviewing can be a bit like attending conferences, in this respect; it is one way you can see where your field is moving.

Peer review and emotional labour

Peer review is the collective labour of deciding which contributions do and don't belong in a particular scholarly conversation. As such, it touches on one of the biggest areas where most people feel vulnerable: belonging. How vulnerable you feel about whether you belong to the particular scholarly community represented by the journal, press, or book series will affect your confidence to review the manuscript and your reaction to reviews as an author. The more personally meaningful the subject of the manuscript, the more vulnerable you may feel in the face of criticism (as an author) or another author's arguments (as a reviewer). The emotional aspects of peer review are not trivial; emotional vulnerability often relates directly to material vulnerability through the ways that publications are used to award jobs, promotions, funding, and so on. Most scholars are contributing to the advancement of knowledge because that knowledge could have meaningful, material effects for some aspect of the way the world works.

Although peer review is part of a collective project of knowledge creation, the process atomizes its participants. The reviewers are not known to each other; they do not sit around a table to discuss manuscripts and come to a consensus on the quality of the contribution, nor what is required to make the manuscript publishable. Anonymity of reviewers and authors to each other (in at least one direction) is normal. The rationale is to enhance objectivity, but it can also serve to dehumanize the other parties and excuse communicative styles that would be unacceptable face to face.

As a reviewer, there is real emotional labour involved in counteracting this potential dehumanization to write supportive and constructive comments. There is also real emotional labour involved in remaining objective and constructive when reading a manuscript that challenges (or ignores) your own contributions to the conversation, or makes a contribution you have not yet published but were hoping to. As an early-career scholar or a newer entrant in a particular conversation, being asked to review may require emotional labour to acknowledge your own expertise and suitability for the job.

As an author, due to the possibility of rejection, emotional labour is required to even submit your manuscript. Your vulnerability around belonging in the conversation will require emotional labour at every step: reading the recommendation, opening the reviewer comments, and reading the reviewer comments. Your emotions need to be addressed before you can get to the intellectual work of figuring out how to revise your manuscript and address the comments. There is an opportunity for the editor to mitigate the amount of emotional labour required – by doing some of the intellectual work of reconciling opposing views, or indicating comments whose content or tone they feel is unwarranted – but this is often not done, even where two reviewers' suggestions are in direct conflict.

For both authors and reviewers, your ability to separate criticism of your work from criticism of your essential self will affect the nature of the emotional work required. Carol Dweck's work on mindsets seems relevant here. The system of peer review, and the value of knowledge production as collective labour, requires a *growth* mindset. Other aspects of contemporary academic cultures tend to reinforce a *fixed* mindset view. Her research has shown that mindset affects how you both give and receive criticism. The key issue is to focus on the work itself and the contribution it makes (or could make) to the scholarly conversation, rather than on the author and their abilities.

Receiving Comments as an Author

This chapter addresses you as an author. Before submission, you made your manuscript as good as you could get it. You sought feedback from critical friends. You may even have hired an editor. The editor or editorial board decides whether to publish your manuscript based on the comments of peer reviewers. The reviewers will have been selected to represent a range of relevant expertise, and none of them may individually be experts in the exact combination of things your manuscript brings together. Although the reviewers and editors do not discuss the manuscript and come to a collective decision, the decision is intended to represent the collective view, taking into account constraints on the total number of manuscripts that can be published. The decision you were aiming for is revise and resubmit. Acceptance without revisions is very uncommon and not to be expected. Rejoice if it happens, but know that it may only happen once or twice in your career.

When you receive your comments, the decision is not up for discussion or debate. Peer review is an editorial process. Reviewers with expertise relevant to your manuscript have taken the time to read and comment on your manuscript. If you are invited to revise and resubmit, I strongly encourage you to do so, unless the required revisions would substantially alter the argument or would require you to do something you consider unethical. You may have to start on the revisions to make this call. If the paper has been rejected, or you decide you can't resubmit to this outlet in good conscience, you should still seriously consider the reviewers' comments as you move forward with the project.

I will address revise-and-resubmit decisions first, beginning with the emotional labour and then moving to the practicalities of the intellectual labour. I'll address the revisions to the manuscript and then the letter to the editor that accompanies the resubmissions. Rejections are dealt with in a separate section following the same pattern: beginning with the emotional and moving to the practicalities.

Emotional work

Receiving your decision and comments is a stark reminder of the vulnerability of submitting. Your manuscript represents years of work. You may be personally invested in the topic or findings. You believe the contribution to knowledge represented by this manuscript is significant. The fact of being published, or being published in this journal or with this press, may be crucial to your ability to secure (in both senses of the word) an academic job or the resources you need to continue this research. You are also busy with other projects, and revising this manuscript is going to disrupt your work plan.

Your manuscript is an individual contribution to a collective conversation. You want to belong (and may already belong) to the community engaged in this conversation. The decision and comments can feel like you are being told you do not belong, inviting your gremlins to bring out their impostor chants. Your gremlins are wrong. Reviewer comments are not about you as a person or your ability as a scholar, even if one of your reviewers has forgotten that and framed their comments as a personal attack. They are comments on this specific manuscript and whether it makes (or could potentially make) a significant contribution to the particular conversations in your field that this journal or press sees itself as contributing to. If your contribution tries to stretch or redraw the boundaries of the conversation, it is even more important to remember that other members of this collective may be attached to the current boundaries and feel threatened by the contribution you are making.

Because of all this, and no matter how often you checked the status of the manuscript on the publisher's portal, it is normal to be somewhat reluctant to actually read the decision. Having read the decision, opening the reviews will take another dose of courage. Procrastination is not a sign that you are weak willed, lazy, or disorganized; it is a response to this emotional vulnerability. If you have other emotionally difficult things going on in your life right now, you may have fewer resources to deal with this particular source of vulnerability.

If you find yourself procrastinating about opening and/or reading the comments, and working up the courage to rip the plaster off doesn't work for you, try one of the following strategies:

- Separate the process of reading and processing the response into a series of small tasks, which don't need to be done consecutively—read the decision, read the editor's comments, skim the reviews, read the first review, etc.
- Open them in the presence of a sympathetic friend so you have emotional support available. Just knowing your friend is available for a phone conversation can help.
- Ask a sympathetic friend or colleague to open the email for you, read the decision, and skim the reviewers' comments. Your friend can then reassure you it is safe to open, or offer to summarize the decision and comments for you to make them easier to absorb.

However you approach it, allow yourself time to experience and process your emotional reaction. Your initial emotional reaction is legitimate. It is absolutely okay to be angry, or sad, or to get up and dance around the room in jubilation. It's unreasonable to assume you can go straight into the practicalities without this. Take a deep breath.

Focus on absorbing the decision first. Feel what you feel. Use the support you need. Some people like to give themselves a time limit for the initial emotional reaction. A day. A week. Long enough to really acknowledge the reaction, but not too long. Then you can take the next step to transition into the practical intellectual work.

Some questions to consider

These questions are intended to help you process your emotional reaction. I encourage you to write out your answers, perhaps longhand in a notebook. You can use them to help you move forward at any stage: before you look at the decision, before you open the review comments, or after you've read the reviewer comments. If they are not helpful, skip this section.

> Can you name the emotion? Does it have a physical manifestation in your body? Can you illustrate how you are feeling?

> What else is going on for you right now that may limit your capacity to deal with the emotions around these reviews?

> What stories are you telling yourself about this decision or the reviews?

If you think of these stories as being told by gremlins (or other imaginary beings that are not you), is there one gremlin? Or are there several? Do you recognize any of them? Do they all agree?

When you look at those stories written out, do you have any evidence that (aspects of) the stories are true? Is there any evidence they may be exaggerated?

Is it possible to let the gremlins argue about this in another room while you get on with the next task? Or, will the gremlins let you try taking the next step as a way of seeing if they are exaggerating?

Given what you've noticed, brainstorm options for taking the next step. Brainstorm names of specific people who might be able to help you.

What are you going to try?

What do you hope will happen?

Practicalities of revising for resubmission

Now that you've dealt with the initial emotional reaction, you need to organize the information in the reviews and make a plan for revising your manuscript. You may have been given a deadline for the revisions, which means you are probably going to have to adjust your other writing and research plans to accommodate this work. If you have coauthors, you may need to organize a meeting to agree a plan, a division of labour, and a timeline.

Make sure you keep a copy of the unrevised version, either by duplicating the document before making revisions or by using the version-control options in your word-processing software to name that version. Having an unrevised version to go back to means you can undo revisions you decide don't work and check that all the reviewers' comments have been addressed. Some journals will go through several rounds of review before acceptance (and possibly even after acceptance), so develop a file-naming convention that helps you keep track and ensures everyone is working on the right document/version. This is particularly important if you are collaborating using software that doesn't allow multiple authors to work in the document at the same time.

You are the author and, as such, you retain control over and responsibility for the final version of the manuscript. You usually have choices about how to address the various editorial comments. Both confidence and humility are required as you make decisions about how to address the reviewers' comments during your revisions. You may want to begin your process by reminding yourself of the contribution you wanted to make and why you thought it was significant. Some of the revisions will require considerable thought, and possibly additional reading or data analysis. Others will be relatively straightforward stylistic changes. You may need to decide between the approaches suggested by different reviewers. Some of the suggestions may seem ludicrous to you, and may be better addressed by clarifying the objective of your paper than by incorporating the reviewers' suggested revisions.

Ideally, you will have a covering note from the editor guiding your reading of the reviewers' comments. This practice is not as common as would be ideal, but if you do have such a note, take it very seriously, even if it's shorter and less detailed than the other documents. The editor's guiding comments can be especially helpful where reviewers clearly disagree with each other or with the decision the editor has communicated to you. The editor should also indicate if there are specific revisions they have agreed must be made for the article to be published. The editor may comment on the tone of reviews and give guidance on comments they think you should take seriously despite the unhelpful tone of a particular review.

You will need to communicate (to the editor, though your note will probably be shared with reviewers of the revision) how you have addressed the reviewers' comments, so it is a good idea to make a list of all the revisions, breaking them down into discrete tasks as much as possible, and keeping a note of which reviewer suggested them. If you make a table, or use a spreadsheet as a table, you can have a column for the reviewer, a column for the comment, and a column to record what you've decided to do about the comment. This makes it easy for you to keep track of what you need to do and helps you write the response to the editor when you resubmit. For coauthored papers, you might add a column for which author has agreed to deal with which comments. A column for noting when revisions have been made in the document can help you track your progress and sort the list to highlight what remains to be done.

You want to cut and paste directly from the reviewers' comments to ensure you have indeed addressed everything. However, it may also be helpful to rewrite the comments in your own words, especially if the tone of the initial review is unhelpful. In some cases, you might even want to ask a friend to reword the comments so you can use what is helpful without the emotional fallout caused by the tone. You are aiming for a working list that does not unnecessarily trigger emotional reactions. If you are using a spreadsheet, create an additional column and then hide the column with the reviewers' words while doing your revisions, unhiding it when you come to write your response to accompany the resubmission. In cases where the tone is not problematic but the reviewer seems to have missed the point, use your decision column to articulate your thinking and record your decision about how to proceed (including decisions not to do anything because the comment is irrelevant).

As you do this, be careful not to focus solely on the negatives. Try not to let your gremlins tell you that you need to decide which reviewers are right and which ones are clearly idiots. They all have valuable expertise to contribute to a collective process. Find the positive comments. If reviewers disagreed, take time to read the most positive review carefully, even if their position was moderated in the final decision.

Is there anything here you can build on?

Can you see where this review complements, rather than contradicts, the others?

Did this review give more attention to things that other reviewers haven't talked about?

Does it comment at all on things other reviewers felt strongly needed improvement?

Decision-making is real intellectual labour and comprises a substantial part of the work involved. Make decisions about the major structural elements first. If you have received a revise-and-resubmit decision, you can assume the editor agreed that your manuscript contained a potentially significant contribution. Approach these questions with that in mind.

Do all the reviewers have the same understanding of the contribution you are trying to make? And does their understanding align with what you think you are trying to do?

Do the reviewers agree this contribution is significant, or could be significant?

Do the reviewers agree you have appropriately located your contribution in relevant scholarly conversations? If they are not agreed on the significance, might this explain why the significance is not clear?

Are all the reviewers convinced the evidence you present supports your argument? If not, do they agree a different argument would make a significant contribution? Do they suggest what additional evidence would be required or what evidence seems to be unnecessary?

Are all the reviewers convinced your evidence is valid, reliable, and complete? If not, what are the specific issues they find problematic?

Would the paper benefit from close revision with attention to sentence flow within paragraphs, word choice, grammar, and punctuation?

You, the reviewers, and the editor all want to improve the manuscript to actually make a significant contribution to the relevant scholarly conversation. Resist the urge to do the small, easy things before you've made decisions about the big, difficult things. Those bigger issues may result in decisions that make other comments irrelevant. You probably want to identify the larger challenges first.

Once you've got the big picture clear, go through the specific suggestions, trying to assign them to particular areas. It is possible that some reviewers have suggested solutions without clarifying the problems, and that their specific suggestions will be redundant if you address the underlying problem in a different way (perhaps suggested by a different reviewer). Some may have provided more extensive comments in the particular area of their expertise. Note whether some issues are dependent on others. Make a note of what kinds of work are required, with a particular focus on work that isn't just rewriting the manuscript.

Do you need to do more reading?

Do you need additional evidence? More data? Additional sources?

Do you need to reanalyze any of the evidence? If so, is this additional work feasible? Do you and your coauthors have the necessary expertise and access to the necessary materials?

This may become another decision point about whether revising and resubmitting this manuscript is a priority right now.

Record all your decisions in your table so you remember them and can communicate them later. Make a plan for doing the work required in as much detail as you can stand. Marking what's already done with a highlighter means your list will fill up with highlighted things, helping you stay motivated by reminding you how far you've come. Once you've made your revisions, have another pass to ensure the article flows well.

At this point, you want to reread the initial reviewers' comments to check you've addressed everything. Remember, "addressed" doesn't mean "done exactly what they suggested". Check your decision notes to make sure you are still happy with your decisions. Make sure you've got notes explaining how the revisions you've made address a particular comment if you have taken a different approach than the one suggested. If you are unsure whether you've addressed everything appropriately, you may want to ask a supportive colleague to check your revised article against the reviewer comments. If you are happy with this version of the manuscript, you are ready to (re)submit.

Resubmitting

When you resubmit your manuscript, you need to include a covering letter responding to the comments. Keep in mind that this is a collective process. The editor made the decision based on the advice of the peer reviewers. Depending on the extent of the revisions required, the editor will either accept the resubmission without sending it out for review again or will send it out for another peer review. Policies differ regarding who reviews resubmissions, but it is usual for at least some of the original reviewers to be asked to review the resubmission. A new reviewer may be brought in at this stage. This means you are addressing your letter to the editor knowing it will probably be shared with the reviewers.

Before composing this letter, remind yourself that the editor wants to publish your work and wants it to be the best it can be. You are not a writer-for-hire writing to a brief; this is *your* manuscript. All writers revise their work based on editor's comments (or even edicts). You need to communicate the decisions you made confidently without seeming arrogant or defensive. Reminding yourself of your common goals for this piece is a good way to get in the right frame of mind. You could even make a list. Definitely take a couple of deep breaths.

Now you are in the right frame of mind, what do you put in this letter? Your goal is to make it easy for the editor (and reviewers) to evaluate how the new version compares to the old. A version of your revision table may be an appropriate means of communicating your decisions to the editor and reviewers. Make sure that what you've written in the decision column is in an acceptable tone, and that you've cleaned the file of any earlier versions that might not be. The editor doesn't need to see the columns you used to assign the work or keep track of your progress. Necessary columns are probably limited to reviewer comment, decision, and what you did (with page references). Direct quotes from the original reviews are preferable to your summary, giving you an opportunity to ensure you didn't misinterpret or miss anything. Depending on the extent of revisions, this letter might be long. You may want to group the comments and revisions by theme or section, especially if that's how you approached the revision process.

If you are new to this, or if you struggled to get into the right frame of mind, ask a colleague with more experience to review your letter for content and tone. Resubmit. Your manuscript may still be rejected at this stage, or further revisions may be necessary. As frustrating as this is, keep in mind that your contribution to the debate will be stronger for all the work you and the reviewers have put into it.

Dealing with a "reject" decision

It happens: Sometimes you send your manuscript off and it gets rejected. A rejection clearly states that this journal or press is not interested in publishing your manuscript. (A revise-and-resubmit decision is not a rejection.) A rejection does not mean your work is unpublishable; it means *this* manuscript is unpublishable in its current form by *this* journal (or press). You may have misjudged the suitability of your work for this outlet, misjudged the readiness of your article, or both. Those are both difficult judgements to make. Everyone gets them wrong sometimes. Take a deep breath.

Your emotional reaction to this decision is valid. Receiving a reject decision is disappointing at best. You may also be angry, confused, or sad. If important career opportunities are dependent on publishing more, or publishing in higher-status outlets, you may feel fear and anxiety. You worked hard on this manuscript. It may be personally meaningful in some way. External validation matters. Allow yourself to feel what you feel. Do whatever you need to do to process the emotions: scream, write angry letters you aren't going to send, journal, vent to a friend, make an appointment with your therapist, etc. The questions in the earlier section on emotional work may be helpful. Then pick yourself up, dust yourself off, learn what you can from this rejection, and make a new plan for this material.

The main difference between a rejection and a revise-and-resubmit decision is that you have an additional decision to make: where to submit a revised version. Unless there is a very clear indication from the editor that they would be interested in a substantially revised version of the manuscript (sometimes called a reject-and-resubmit decision), you should assume not to resubmit to this particular outlet. One common strategy for managing the emotional impact of a rejection is to choose a backup journal (or press) when you make your initial decision about where to submit. If you did this, review your decision criteria in the light of any feedback you received and either confirm or adjust this decision. Otherwise, I've gone into more detail about the issue of fit and journal selection in another volume in this series, *Scholarly Publishing*. I also recommend Pat Thomson and Barbara Kamler's chapter on understanding the discourse community in which a journal is located in their book *Writing for Peer Reviewed Journals*, or Week Four of Wendy Belcher's *Writing Your Journal Article in 12 Weeks*. I do not recommend starting with a general list of high-ranking journals in your field. Start with the audience. Bring the rankings in only once you've identified journals that address that audience. I recommend making a decision about where you will submit first, even if the manuscript needs substantial revision.

Once you have decided where you will submit, you will then need to decide whether the manuscript can be submitted to the new outlet as it stands or whether some revision is necessary. A rejection is often the result of the editor deciding the revisions required are too substantial to warrant a revise-and-resubmit decision. You will need to make a judgement about whether that was partly due to your error in judgement about which journal to submit to, or whether substantial revisions are required. If you use the reviewer comments in making your revisions, you should acknowledge the anonymous reviewers in a footnote to your new submission.

You may have considerably less editorial feedback for a rejection than you would for a revise-and-resubmit decision. Due to the large volume of manuscripts received and the difficulty of securing reviewers, many journals have a system for screening submissions before sending them out for review, so as not to waste reviewers' time on manuscripts that are clearly not suited to the journal's focus or not up to the minimum standard. This type of rejection, often referred to as a "desk reject," should be communicated relatively quickly. You've not lost a lot of time, but you don't have a lot of information to help you improve your judgement either. Pay attention to any comments the editor makes, even if they seem formulaic. Make sure you didn't miss some basic things before you submitted.

> Did you consider the particular audience and conversation this journal or press engages?

Did you follow the published guidelines for authors with regards to length, style, and format?

Did you ensure the general structure of your manuscript was in line with what is usually published by this outlet (e.g. the relative length of different sections)?

Was your manuscript copy-edited and proofread before submission?

If your answer to any of these questions is no, it is possible that addressing these basic issues before submitting to another journal is sufficient. It may be prudent to discuss your decisions with a colleague with more experience publishing in this field, or even to ask a colleague to comment on your manuscript prior to submission.

If your manuscript has gone out for review and then been rejected, you have some confirmation that your judgements about fit and quality were reasonable. While it will have taken longer for this decision to be made and communicated, you have the additional benefit of reviewers' reports. A manuscript can be rejected at any point in the process. While it is frustrating to have your manuscript rejected after one or more rounds of revision, the journal was not blithely wasting your time (or that of the reviewers). There are good reasons you got as far as you did.

Peer review is an editorial process. The comments of these expert reviewers will help you make decisions about what to do next. You never have to slavishly respond to every comment, and this is even more clear in the case of a rejection. The reviewers had a particular journal or press in mind when writing their comments. Since you will not be resubmitting a revised version to this same outlet, your first step is to sort out the reasons you were rejected from this journal from comments that might be relevant regardless of where you resubmit. The tips in the earlier section on the practicalities of revising for resubmission should be helpful.

Giving Feedback Constructively as a Reviewer

This chapter addresses you as a reviewer. Although very early in your career you may primarily be on the receiving end of peer review, once you've published you will probably be asked to be a reviewer. As you advance in your career, demands to review will likely increase. You may also serve on editorial boards, and even as an editor, at some point in your career.

When taking on the role of peer reviewer, keep in mind that you are contributing to the collective process of shaping the field and the discipline, as well as ensuring the quality of scholarship within it. You are not the only reviewer of this manuscript. You may have been invited to review based on a specific area of expertise relevant to the manuscript. Your review will be considered by an editor or editorial board alongside the other reviews, and the editor will make the final decision about whether to publish this manuscript. In addition to this role advising the editor, your comments to the author are a form of editorial feedback, similar to that provided by professional editors in other types of publishing. Whether or not this manuscript will be accepted for publication, your comments are an opportunity to contribute to the improvement of scholarship in your field through asynchronous, usually anonymous, mentorship.

The structure of this chapter is similar to the structure of the previous chapter. I will begin with a consideration of the emotional issues before turning to the practicalities. The practical issues for reviewers fall into two main categories. I begin by addressing the question of how to fit reviewing into your already-demanding workload. Then I turn my attention to writing a recommendation to the editor and writing reviews that are both rigorous and supportive.

Emotional work

Despite considerable debate about the role of emotions in making objective evaluations, and whole bodies of scholarly work on objectivity in research, academic culture tends to try to avoid emotions. They aren't supposed to influence our judgements. And yet they do. Denying the existence or effect of emotions often makes things worse. Noticing your emotional response can be a useful step in reviewing a paper. Your emotions can guide you towards things you want to consider more fully. Considering the emotional impact of your review can help you craft it so that it is useful to the author. You need not communicate this emotional reaction, or the processing of it, to either the editor or the author, but it is an important step in the process.

At first glance, being a reviewer appears to be a much less vulnerable role than that of an author submitting a manuscript. After all, you don't risk rejection in quite the same way. The very fact of being invited suggests you belong to this particular community of scholars, at least in the mind of the editor. That won't necessarily stop your gremlins from shouting "impostor!" and coming up with a long list of reasons the editor must have sent the invitation to review in error or desperation. If you currently have a manuscript under review with the journal sending the request, you may even have a gremlin who thinks acceptance of your paper is dependent on your review of this one.

Your gremlins are wrong. Loud but wrong. Take a deep breath and remind yourself you have been invited to review because you have relevant expertise. Usually, this expertise is demonstrated by having published in that field. Occasionally, those actively researching in an area but not yet published may be asked to review, perhaps after being recommended by a colleague. Take a moment to clarify what specific expertise prompted the editor to invite you. Sometimes editors misunderstand your expertise, or make assumptions that may not be valid, but do not mistake your own false modesty for an editorial error. There are good reasons they asked you. Take another deep breath.

One of the paradoxes of peer review in an increasingly competitive academic context is that you are engaged in a review process focused on shaping the scholarly conversation, but are aware that the outcome of the review process will affect the author's ability to continue to do scholarly work and contribute to that conversation. As a peer, that scholar may also be a competitor for funding, jobs, and other resources necessary to participate in the conversation. Publishers have conflict-of-interest policies to address the potential misuse of the review process to either advance or frustrate the career ambitions of scholars for reasons other than the quality of the work you've been asked to review. Beyond clear conflicts of interest, this context may trigger your own vulnerability when you review. The first question to ask in relation to your reaction to a manuscript is whether this is a problem with the manuscript itself or whether something is triggering your own insecurities. You share with the author the ability to learn from this process and become a better scholar.

In addition to feeling vulnerable about whether you belong to the community of experts, the review itself is a form of writing that will be seen by the editor and other reviewers. You are one of two or three reviewers. You are not anonymous to all of these people, and they are also your peers. You may be concerned that your review will confirm you should never have been asked, or that you are considered too harsh or too lenient in your review and recommendations, or that the comments you make will cause the editor and other reviewers to rethink their opinion of your published work. You may feel more vulnerable in these ways if reviewing in an open review system where the author will (eventually) know who wrote the review. Your gremlins may exaggerate these fears, but they are not entirely irrational.

Being a reviewer can also trigger the vulnerability you feel as an author. Your author-self may have strong opinions about what reviewers should say and how they should say it. You may feel reluctant to criticize the manuscript knowing how much work will have gone into it. You may be tempted to downplay your criticisms or couch them in ambiguous language. This will not be helpful. A growth mindset is crucial to the process of peer review for both author and reviewer. Your expert comments will support the growth of this scholar and their programme of research.

In particular, judgements about readiness for submission are incredibly difficult to make. As an author, you may struggle to make these judgements about readiness and writing style. As a reviewer, you see how others have made those judgements. The quality of the writing may not match the quality of the research and scholarship. English is not the most common first language of scholars. In many disciplines, English is the dominant language of scholarly debate, and even where there is considerable scholarly publishing in other languages, publishing in English enables authors to reach a wider range of readers.

Your initial reaction is an indicator of your personal standards. Your emotional reaction to the manuscript may be directed inwards or towards the author (or the editor who sent the manuscript out for review). Anger, annoyance, or disappointment can be indicators of unexamined assumptions. Reflecting on that emotional reaction can help you devise strategies for responding constructively. Acknowledging and naming the reaction may help you articulate your standards clearly – an important element in providing constructive feedback. It also allows you to calibrate your personal standard. A good desk-rejection process should weed out most of the manuscripts that really would be a waste of your time. If you find yourself annoyed at the low quality of submissions, you may be expecting too much. Some revision is expected at this stage.

Some questions to consider

These questions are intended to help you process your emotional reaction. I encourage you to write out your answers, perhaps longhand in a notebook. If they are not helpful, skip this section.

> What is your initial reaction to the manuscript (or request to review)? Note it without judgement.

> Can you name the emotion? Does it have a physical manifestation in your body? Can you illustrate how you are feeling?

Is this emotion directed at yourself or at someone else? If someone else, who?

Is anything else going on for you right now that may limit your capacity for generosity (to yourself or to the author)? Noticing (and noting) this context may be helpful in and of itself.

Is your reaction focused on the person or the manuscript itself? If your initial reaction (or part of it) is focused on the person, can you identify specific elements of the manuscript that triggered that personal reaction?

Are you concerned about how the author might receive your criticisms? What stories are you telling yourself about the author's reaction? Which elements of those stories are under your control?

Based on the notes you have taken in response to these questions, what practical steps might you take to ensure your feedback is constructive?

Do you have any additional comments you want to make (confidentially) to the editor?

Workload and responding to requests to review

Participating in peer review is crucial to the whole system of scholarly publishing and relies on diffuse reciprocity. From fairly early in your academic career, reviewing manuscripts is a normal part of your workload. Because you have no control over when you get asked to review, it's hard to build in time for this work; and yet, when you do get asked, you are required to complete the work promptly. It can end up feeling like reviewing manuscripts is always stealing time and effort from your research and teaching, or constitutes an overload, creating a certain amount of resentment even among those who really value this work. In this section, I'll discuss general considerations for deciding how much of this work to do and how to fit it into your workload.

One way to manage the time and effort you put into reviewing manuscripts is to quantify your commitment to diffuse reciprocity. Calculate how many manuscripts you submit on average in a year. Multiply by the average number of reviewers required to review your manuscripts. Use this number as a rough guide to how much time you need to allow in your schedule for reviewing. You cannot control when requests come in, but you can keep some slack in your schedule to enable you to say "yes" when you do receive a request. This means not overcommitting to other research deadlines – which is easier said than done, especially in a culture that makes you feel like you are never producing enough. If you block time for reviewing every month, and then don't receive a request, you can always fill that time with other work. It is better for your own mental and physical health, and for your reputation, to undercommit and overdeliver.

If the number of requests you receive exceeds your guideline number, you may decide further criteria for triaging review requests. You may further specify your expertise, turning down requests that are bordering on tangential or in which you are no longer actively keeping up with developments. You could limit yourself to a particular set of journals in your field, based on criteria that are important to you. Some scholars have decided to support their commitment to open access and the affordability of scholarly publications by boycotting journals published by particular commercial publishers, for example. This type of decision should not be used as a way to reduce your commitment to diffuse reciprocity. Instead, reallocate the reviewing time to publishers whose practices you support.

If, despite having published in your field, you are not getting requests, or not getting requests from the journals you'd like to review for, you may want to be a bit more proactive. Some journals accept offers to review. There may be an application form on the journal's website, or you can email the editor outlining your areas of expertise. It seems that many journals rely heavily on the editor's own networks (and those of their editorial board). Journals sometimes organize events at conferences; these may offer opportunities to meet editorial board members and signal a willingness to review. Make sure that colleagues know you are willing to review and what your expertise is. It is common to suggest alternate reviewers when turning down a request.

When you receive a request to review, you should take all reasonable steps to ensure the author is not waiting an unreasonable amount of time for a decision on their manuscript. Taking the time to consider the request and make a decision within one working day of receiving it is not unreasonable. Responding quickly is especially important if you are not able to undertake the review on this occasion. The sooner the editor receives your refusal, the sooner they can ask someone else. Not responding at all is unacceptably rude and introduces unnecessary delays while the editor waits for your reply before inviting someone else.

Two criteria must be met before you accept a review: You must have the necessary expertise, and you must have the time to complete the review promptly.

There are good reasons you have been asked to do this review, so it is highly likely you have the necessary expertise. If you have changed your research focus and the request is based on work you published many years ago in a field you no longer keep up with, you may want to refuse on these grounds. If it seems the editor has made an error, first ask yourself if you have any expertise relevant to the manuscript. You are not the only reviewer, and may have been asked because of specific expertise, even though there are other aspects of the manuscript about which you know nothing. It's okay if you know the scholarship on this topic but are not familiar with the particular methodology, theoretical framework, data set, sources, or geographic location used (or if you are not familiar with the general literature but are an expert in the methodology, theoretical framework, data set, sources, or geographic location). You can clarify the scope of your expertise in your response, if necessary, and limit your comments accordingly.

You should always look at your calendar and your to-do list to confirm you have the time before you reply. If the request specifies a preferred turnaround time, look at your existing commitments and make a realistic decision about whether you can review it in that time. If you can't do it by the requested deadline, but could complete it within two weeks of that date, consider requesting a different deadline as a condition of your acceptance. If no turnaround time is suggested, use four to six weeks as your window. I strongly recommend you estimate the time required and actually block that time in your calendar. You probably need two or three blocks of time: one to read the manuscript and make some initial notes; one to draft your review; and one to review your draft and make any revisions before sending it. You may need to move something else, but time is not going to magically appear. If you don't use time blocking to organize your work, look at your existing to-do list and deadlines for other commitments. What will have to be given lower priority if you say "yes"? If you can't block the time in your calendar, or drop something else down your to-do list to prioritize this review, you should turn it down. Yes, everybody is busy. Saying yes and then not doing the review by the deadline is not helpful. If you never have time to review, you need to review your priorities more generally.

If you are confident of your expertise, and that you can complete the review in the time requested, your reply will be short and sweet. You may also give a conditional acceptance of the request. It is then up to the editor to accept your conditions. If the journal does not provide reviewer guidelines, you may request them or ask for guidance on specific questions that concern you.

If the answer is no (for whatever reason), then say "no" as soon as possible. Do not delay replying because you feel bad about saying "no." Diffuse reciprocity means you have an obligation to review manuscripts, but you don't have to review this manuscript. "No" is a complete sentence. You need not apologize. You certainly do not need to go into a long explanation of how many requests you get and how busy you are. Everyone is busy. The editor gets it. It is helpful to clarify your expertise, especially if this is your grounds for refusal, and to indicate whether you are willing to be asked again in future. It is also helpful to suggest other scholars who may be a good fit for the article, especially if they are unlikely to be known to the editor. Indicate why you think they would be appropriate, with reference to a publication, conference paper, or other evidence that you know their work.

It may be appropriate to recommend that a postdoctoral fellow or doctoral candidate you supervise might review the paper. In this case, where the person you plan to recommend has a direct relationship with you, it is advisable to discuss it with them first. You may offer to mentor them through the process if they have not reviewed manuscripts before, giving them guidance on how to approach the task and reading and commenting on the review before they submit. If they are happy to have their name put forward, propose this to the editor, indicating both the expertise of the person you are recommending and any support you plan to provide. The decision remains with the editor.

The decision should not take long to make. You don't have to resolve all the emotions triggered by being asked in order to reply. It's okay to feel nervous, especially if you haven't done many reviews before. Experience will help you be more confident. This is one situation where the default can be yes (especially if you don't receive many requests). Check your calendar and to-do list. Reply. Then line up the support you need to do the job. That might be as simple as having coffee with a colleague to ask them how they approach manuscript reviews and how much time they usually take.

While you are making plans, be kind to your future self. There is a good chance that the manuscript will require revision and another round of review. Consider the policy of this specific journal, and your own timeline for the first review, to estimate when you might receive revisions. Build in capacity to review the revisions. Even a reminder in your planner or calendar that revisions might come back will help you make better decisions about other opportunities that arise in the meantime. If the manuscript is rejected (or accepted without the need for further review) you can reallocate that time.

Making a recommendation to the editor

When reviewing the manuscript, you need to keep in mind both functions of peer review. You are not only making a recommendation to the editor about whether this manuscript should be published but also providing editorial feedback to the author. You might want to read through the manuscript once quickly to get an overall sense and decide on your recommendation, then read more closely with a view to providing helpful comments to the author.

The form for your comments may separate the two functions, with a section for confidential comments to the editor and another section for your general review. There may also be checkboxes for the overall recommendation. The editor will read all of your comments. The comments directed to the editor should be addressed primarily to the question of whether you recommend publication or rejection, and which revisions you deem crucial. This is also where you can communicate any criticisms you have of the process.

Since you are not making the decision, but are one of several reviewers advising the editor, you should also be clear about the reasons for your recommendation in your comments to the editor. It is highly unlikely that all of the reviewers will agree. The editor needs to adjudicate among the recommendations and determine whether the revisions necessary to satisfy the concerns of some of the reviewers would be reasonable or whether, given the number of submissions, the manuscript requires too much work to be worth a revise-and-resubmit decision. Furthermore, if your expertise is stronger in some areas and weaker in others, the editors will be balancing reviews with different areas of expertise. It needs to be clear whether the elements of the manuscript within your area of expertise meet minimum standards of rigour – and, if not, whether the flaws are reparable.

It is particularly important to be clear about the relationship between this contribution and the focus of the specific journal, book series, or publisher's list to which it has been submitted. Assume that, if the editor sent it out for review, there is some reason to think it might be appropriate. Specify what makes it appropriate or inappropriate for this particular venue, in your view. If you think this manuscript should be accepted (with or without revisions) despite taking the journal into new territory, some specific reasons why you think this new territory is appropriate will be helpful.

You don't have to repeat the details you provide in the part of your review that the author will see. It will be helpful to highlight those issues that are most important to your recommendation.

Giving feedback constructively

Although peer review is editorial labour, it is not the only editorial feedback an author should receive. The author should have sought feedback from critical friends and had the paper copy-edited and proofread before submission. Your role is equivalent to that of an agent or editor for trade-published authors, but without the benefit of an ongoing personal relationship that might temper harsh comments. Your goal is to contribute to the advancement of knowledge in your field by providing comments that will improve scholarship.

Being rigorous and supportive in your review does not mean you cannot limit the time and effort you put into this task. Keep your goals as a reviewer in mind. A concise review may be more effective than a long one – as long as it provides the editor with a clear recommendation, supported with a justification, and provides the author with clear advice about how their contribution can be strengthened. While you want to be thorough in your review, if your comments are too long and detailed, the author will struggle to use them effectively to improve their work. It is also important to distinguish improving this manuscript from general comments about the author's programme of research as a whole.

Kindness begins with acknowledging your own emotional reactions and making sure you are not projecting unreasonable things onto this author. Questioning your desire to make snarky comments will give you clues as to how to transform them into something more constructive. Your review should not contain attacks on the author. It should focus on the quality of the work. If you think this manuscript is so awful it is not worth your time and effort, direct your criticism to the editor, suggesting their desk-rejection practices and/or criteria for reviewer selection could be improved. The author is guilty of nothing more than poor judgement about the readiness of their manuscript for review.

Your focus will be primarily on the big issues. You may need to read the manuscript more than once. Begin with your overall comments about the contribution to knowledge and quality of the piece. It is helpful to summarize what you understand the contribution to knowledge to be and to say something specific about its value. This is also where you get to say encouraging things about the contribution – even if the paper as it stands needs a *lot* of work. Similarly, if you think there is no contribution to knowledge, you should specify why you think that – where this has already been done, why it is not a useful replication or confirmation of existing work, etc.

Then make comments about specific sections of the manuscript. Expectations will vary by discipline, and the overall structure and level of detail in each section will vary by journal. Comment on the strengths as well as the weaknesses. Your comments should support your recommendation and indicate clearly both why you think this manuscript is worth revising and how much revision is required to make it publishable. If you are recommending rejection, point out what, if anything, is interesting (if not anywhere near fully enough developed). If you are only qualified to speak to some areas of the manuscript, you should be clear about those limitations and signal the focus of your review. Assume one of the other reviewers has strengths in the areas of your weaknesses.

The author gets to make choices about their work. Knowing that the author will receive other reviews alongside your own makes it even more important to keep this in mind as you write. Be clear about the problem you have identified before suggesting potential solutions. There may be more than one legitimate way to approach a problem. You don't need to specify the solution, but clarity about any problems and their gravity makes it much easier for the author to make appropriate decisions and find solutions. If there is a clear connection between the revisions you are suggesting and the problem they will address, the author is more likely to find your suggestion helpful and will have more information at their disposal if your suggestion is incompatible with the suggestion of another reviewer.

Questions can be helpful. When something crucial is unclear in the manuscript, you need to make assumptions about the author's intentions in order to suggest revisions. Phrasing your assumption as a question may be useful in this situation, especially if you can also indicate what makes you think this is their intent. Similarly, if something is missing that you expect to see, you have no way of knowing whether that information is not available or whether the author didn't realize its relevance. Ask if the author has these details and indicate how they would strengthen the manuscript if included.

Critique includes positive comments. Even if you think the manuscript doesn't need revision, it is statistically unlikely that the other reviewers and editors will agree. Clearly identifying the strengths of the paper will help the author reconcile praise with critical comments should they be asked to make revisions. Where your review is less glowing, the revisions you suggest will enable the author to build on what is done well. Everyone has a tendency to amplify the negative and minimize the positive, so it's a good idea to begin with a clear statement of the positive aspects of the manuscript, and remind the author of why you think it is worth the effort to revise in your final paragraph.

Although the author has choices, there will be some issues which you consider compulsory. Be very clear about what is crucial to make this a publishable contribution, and what is optional but would strengthen the contribution. Peer review is not a place for the fine art of understatement. Do not "suggest" unless what you are suggesting is truly optional. Similarly, do not think it rude to state the obvious. What is obvious to you may not be obvious to the author. Making them guess at things you could have specified is not constructive. For example, if the conclusions are not fully supported by the evidence presented, the author has a choice to include more evidence or to modify their conclusions to be more reasonable in the light of the evidence presented. If the latter course of action would mean the contribution to knowledge is not significant enough to warrant publication, this needs to be clear. It may also be worth explicitly stating that a less ambitious conclusion would still make a significant contribution, if this is the case.

A recurring frustration of authors when revising for resubmission is the word limit. If you are recommending additional information of some kind, you might also consider whether there is something obvious that is superfluous to the author's objectives. All research prompts further questions; while it is valuable to acknowledge these as evidence of the significance of the contribution, be careful not to suggest that these further questions need to be addressed to make the current manuscript publishable. This manuscript represents one article (or monograph) in a larger body of work coming out of the author's programme of research. It cannot do everything. The questions are, does it do something that makes a contribution, and does it do it well enough?

Once you've made your main substantive comments, you might want to consider the manuscript from the perspective of a busy reader. Skimming is an essential academic skill. Is the main contribution understandable to the reader who reads the introduction, headings, and conclusion? Are there any revisions to the structure, or to the introduction or conclusion, that would make it clearer?

At this stage in the process, the manuscript is unlikely to be ready for detailed copy-editing. Copy-editing issues need to be fixed before final submission, but the substantive issues of structure, evidence, and suitable engagement with the literature need to be addressed first. There is no point making a sentence pretty if it's going to be cut altogether. It is helpful to point out items that need to be added to the author's editing checklist, especially if you are reviewing a resubmission, but give the revision comments more weight (unless the only reason the manuscript is unpublishable in its current form is poor copy-editing).

That said, it would be appropriate to indicate any major recurring issues of style, especially if these affect the persuasiveness of the argument. For example, you might flag problems with referencing, in conjunction with substantive comments about the engagement with relevant literatures. Lack of clarity about the argument or evidence may be affected by poor sentence or paragraph structure. Choices regarding discipline- or field-specific language (sometimes disparagingly referred to as "jargon") may contribute to a lack of clarity about the contribution, argument, or evidence. Some authors will be L2 English speakers and may have minor style issues you could point out in a general way.

It is a good idea to keep a copy of your comments. You will want to refer to them if you are asked to review a resubmission and editors do not always send them with the resubmission. Good practice in privacy and data protection suggests deleting any copies of your comments and the manuscript once it has been accepted or rejected.

Reviewing a resubmission

When a manuscript is resubmitted after revisions it is normal practice to send it out to the original reviewers, unless the revisions were minor. In some cases a new reviewer may be sought at this stage, perhaps because one of the original reviewers is unable to review. The editor will usually also share all of the original reviews and the author's reply with you. A quick turnaround is even more important at this stage. You should make every effort to find the time, if you did not block it off when you first reviewed the manuscript. If you need to take longer than the editor would like, communicate that promptly and agree an alternative deadline.

The primary question you need to answer is: "Is this publishable?" Even if further refinement is necessary to answer that question in the affirmative, no *new* issues should be introduced at this stage. Check with the editor to confirm whether there is an expectation that reviewers provide detailed copy-editing comments. Journal practice varies in this area, and many will either hire a copy editor or consider copy editing to be part of the editor's role.

Emotionally, this stage of the process may require you to accept an editorial decision that was contrary to your initial recommendation. You will also need to acknowledge differences of opinion among reviewers and make tough decisions about the importance of your own recommendations for revisions in comparison to those of other reviewers, especially where these are incompatible. Your vulnerability around acceptable standards and belonging (as a scholar in this community or as a reviewer) may be triggered. You may also be legitimately frustrated by the apparent lack of respect your comments were given by the author or editors. Use the questions after the earlier section on emotional work to help you process your emotional reaction and decide how to proceed. It may be appropriate to communicate confidentially with the editor about your frustrations, either to seek clarity or to express concerns about the process.

Your comments will focus primarily on whether the comments on the previous version have been adequately addressed. The author may have addressed your concerns in a different way than you suggested. They will also have had to reconcile the comments of multiple reviewers, perhaps choosing between incompatible suggestions. The author's decisions should be documented in the accompanying letter to the editor, so make sure you read that before finalizing your comments. If the author's attempt to address all of the comments has made things worse, you might suggest a way forward that works better, or clarify the essential elements in light of others' concerns.

Your comments to the author are not the place to get into an argument (or a stand-off) with another reviewer. The author does not need to agree with your position in major theoretical or methodological debates in your field to be published. They need to meet the current standards and make a contribution to the debate. If necessary, communicate your concerns about another reviewer's comments to the editor confidentially.

It is also important to read through the whole manuscript with a bit of distance to ensure it remains coherent following revisions. You might also check that a busy reader skimming the text with a focus on introduction, subheadings, and conclusions would get a clear sense of the contribution. Be careful not to introduce issues not raised in the original reviews. The goal of the process is to either publish the contribution or confirm that the amount of work required to make a publishable contribution is too great. If further revisions are required, they should be focused on refinement of a specific issue (raised in the first round) or general but minor revisions for clarity.

Conclusion: Peer Review Supports the Advancement of Knowledge

Despite valid criticisms of peer review as a system, it is crucial to the advancement of knowledge and the protection of academic freedom. Participating in peer review – as an author, a reviewer, a member of an editorial board, or an editor – ensures your scholarly peers' values play an important role in publishing decisions. Done well, peer review also provides important editorial feedback that improves the quality of knowledge. Being edited is difficult. Providing editorial feedback constructively is a skill you can develop. It is crucial to acknowledge and address your emotional reactions, and to focus on the work rather than the person. Everyone involved in these processes is capable of making significant contributions to knowledge. Peer review supports them in doing so.

Notes and Further Reading

What is Peer Review?

The quotation from Aileen Fyfe et al. can be found on page 12 of *Untangling Academic Publishing: A history of the relationship between commercial interests, academic prestige and the circulation of research* (2017, DOI 10.5281/zenodo.546100, open access).

I use the term "scholarly conversation" rather than field, discipline, or similar terms because decisions about publications are usually focused on the more limited scope covered by a particular journal, book series, or press.

Although all editors and reviewers are collectively engaged in creating and maintaining the boundaries of their particular conversation, the rigidity of the boundaries varies from one journal to another. Pat Thomson provides a useful description of rigid boundaries (with a focus on the early-career academic author) in "When peer review is scent marking" (June 19, 2017, *Patter*, patthomson.net/2017/06/19/when-peer-review-is-scent-marking/).

This blog post by Kris Wissoker, of Duke University Press, clarified some things for me about peer review and alerted me to the role the press may play in assisting authors to respond to peer reviewer comments: "Editorial Director Ken Wissoker on why he loves peer review" (September 14, 2017, *News from Duke University Press*, dukeupress.wordpress.com/2017/09/14/editorial-director-ken-wissoker-on-why-he-loves-peer-review/). Clients have confirmed they have received such support from other university presses. Conversations with scholars who publish books suggest there may be considerable variation among publishers in how much support is available and from whom.

The comparison to professional editorial labour in traditional publishing is illustrated by Thomas E. Ricks, "The book he wasn't supposed to write" (August 22, 2017, *The Atlantic*, www.theatlantic.com/entertainment/archive/2017/08/the-secret-life-of-a-book-manuscript/536982/). I suspect many academic readers will identify with the frustration and anger expressed, the work involved in revisions, and the ultimate acceptance of the value of even harsh criticism.

The payment of an honorarium (in cash or in kind) for reviewing book manuscripts does not change the voluntary nature of the task.

Publons includes an initiative for training peer reviewers (Publons.com/community/academy/), using experienced mentors and a short online curriculum. This initiative appears to be designed to both improve the quality of peer review and increase the size of the reviewer pool.

One example of the questioning of high profits and demand for reduced prices is the periodic demand for a boycott of Elsevier, one of the main commercial publishers of academic journals. Some universities have also taken the decision to stop subscribing to Elsevier journals due to cost (among other reasons), which is sometimes presented as a boycott but may be a rational budget decision. See, for example, "University of California boycotts publishing giant Elsevier over journal costs and open access" (February 28, 2019 *Science*, www.sciencemag.org/news/2019/02/university-california-boycotts-publishing-giant-elsevier-over-journal-costs-and-open) or "Europe expanded the "No Elsevier Deal" zone & this could change everything" (July 30, 2018, Hilda Bastien, PLOS, blogs.plos.org/absolutely-maybe/2018/07/30/europe-expanded-the-no-elsevier-deal-zone-this-could-change-everything/).

New publishing ventures arising in response to the critique of commercial publishers' involvement in academic publishing include The Open Library of the Humanities, www.openlibhums.org. For more on open-access scholarly publishing, see Peter Suber, "A very brief introduction to open access", legacy.earlham.edu/~peters/fos/brief.htm, and the list of references he maintains.

In an effort to counter the lack of recognition of peer-review labour, Publons (publons.com) enables you to keep a record of it and verifies this record through partnerships with publishers. This does not resolve the question of whether it really counts for whoever you submit your verified record to.

For more on vulnerability and belonging, you might find the work of Brené Brown helpful. Brené Brown, *Daring Greatly: How the Courage to be Vulnerable Transforms the Way We Live, Love, Parent and Lead* (2012, Penguin Random House).

Carol Dweck's work on mindset includes strategies for shifting from a fixed mindset, in which you believe your work is a reflection of your innate intelligence and ability, to a growth mindset, in which you acknowledge that you are always learning and growing. Carol S. Dweck, *Mindset: Changing the Way You Think to Fulfil Your Potential* (revised edition, 2017, Robinson).

My approach to emotions is also influenced by principles of mindfulness, which I have learned in a somewhat disjointed way from various sources. Jennifer Hofmann's *How to Organize Anything* (available to download here: jenniferhofmann.com/books/organizing-clutter/) has been particularly influential in how I apply these principles practically. The goal is not to change your emotional reaction; the goal is awareness of the emotions, and their impact on your actions, so that you can act in alignment with your values.

Receiving Comments as an Author

I use the term "gremlins" to refer to the voices in your head, which others may refer to as "inner critic," "negative mind chatter," or similar. I prefer this type of approach over the quasi-medicalization inherent in terms like "impostor syndrome." Attributing some of this internal dialogue to personas separate from yourself can help you get enough distance to evaluate the truth of the statements and engage strategies to move forward. My own position was influenced initially by Havi Brooks, of The Fluent Self (fluentself.com), who uses the term "monsters." Helen Kara suggests some useful strategies in "Ten ways to reduce negative mind chatter" (February 21, 2019, helenkara.com/2019/02/21/ten-ways-to-reduce-negative-mind-chatter/).

Helen Kara has written about the emotional work of waiting for peer reviews. "Is peer review bad for your mental health?" (March 27, 2018, helenkara.com/2018/03/27/is-peer-review-bad-for-your-mental-health/; also published at *LSE Impact Blog* on April 19, 2018, blogs.lse.ac.uk/impactofsocialsciences/2018/04/19/is-peer-review-bad-for-your-mental-health/).

Charlotte Lieberman's article, "Why you procrastinate (it has nothing to do with self-control)" (March 25,

2019, *New York Times*, www.nytimes.com/2019/03/25/smarter-living/why-you-procrastinate-it-has-nothing-to-do-with-self-control.html), provides an overview of the relationship between procrastination and emotions, and includes links to academic research.

If you do not have a colleague who is willing or able to open your reviewer comments for you, or you are feeling too vulnerable to ask, I offer this as a paid service: "Reviewer Comments Procrastination Buster" (JoVanEvery.ca/reviewer-comments-procrastination-buster).

When processing emotions, it can be helpful to be able to name them. This is often not as easy as it seems. *The Emotion Thesaurus* (Becca Puglisi & Angela Ackerman, 2018, JADD Publishing) is written as a resource for writers, and thus includes common physical sensations associated with emotions. There are also several lists of feelings available from coaches and therapists. I like the feelings and needs list, and the feelings and interpretations list, from Wise Heart (an interpersonal communications coach): www.wiseheartpdx.org/handouts.

My recommendations for how to address the reviewer comments have been influenced by several sources. My general approach has been influenced by Liz Lerman's *Critical Response Process*, further details of which are in the notes to the following chapter. Matthew Paterson shared his strategy, which I published on my website in 2014: "Managing manuscript edits" (jovanevery.ca/managing-manuscript-edits/). I've since added links to several other sources of advice, including Raul Pacheco-Vega's "How to respond to reviewer comments: the drafts review matrix" (June 23, 2016, www.raulpacheco.org/2016/06/how-to-respond-to-reviewer-comments-the-drafts-review-matrix/), Helen Kara's "How to deal with reviewers' comments" (May 31, 2018, helenkara.com/2018/05/31/how-to-deal-with-reviewers-comments/), and Tanya Golash-Boza's "How to respond to a 'revise and resubmit' from an academic journal: Ten steps to a successful revision" (March 18, 2011, getalifephd.blogspot.com/2011/03/how-to-respond-to-revise-and-resubmit.html). I also recommend Chapter 7, "Engaging with reviewers and editors", of Pat Thomson and Barbara Kamler's *Writing for Peer Reviewed Journals: Strategies for getting published* (2013, Routledge) and "Week X: Revising and Resubmitting Your Article" of Wendy Laura Belcher's *Writing Your Journal Article in Twelve Weeks* (2nd Edition, 2019, University of Chicago Press).

My suggestions for getting into the right frame of mind for writing the letter to the editor to accompany your resubmission draw heavily on Havi Brooks, "Awkward conversations (and a wacky exercise)" (November 10, 2008, *Fluent Self*, www.fluentself.com/blog/habits/awkward-conversations-wacky-exercise/). Melissa Dalgliesh's "Learning to love being edited" (April 6,

2017, *Hook & Eye*, hookandeye.ca/2017/04/06/learning-to-love-being-edited/) may also help you figure out why this is difficult for you.

The situation around rejections and resubmitting to the same journal has changed somewhat over the past few years. It seems that, due to the high number of submissions and limits on how many articles can be published per issue, the bar for a revise-and-resubmit decision has risen. Many journals also have a strict desk-rejection policy to make better use of their reviewer pool. If your rejection is accompanied by a note from the editor clearly indicating they may be willing to consider a new submission on this topic at some point in the future, you may be able to resubmit to this journal. This decision is being referred to as "reject and resubmit." If this happens to you, get advice from someone senior in your field to make sure you have understood the decision correctly and your gremlins aren't interpreting a revise and resubmit as a rejection. If it is a reject, I suggest you consider this kind of thing exactly the same way as a regular reject. They are not willing to accept this manuscript, and the revisions required are too substantial to warrant a revise-and-resubmit decision. It will require major work. There is no timeline. There is no need to reply to the comments. The only difference is that you can consider sending it back to them if you want to.

Making substantial revisions following a reject decision may mean going back to an earlier stage in the writing process. Other *Short Guides* in this series will be helpful. *Scholarly Publishing* has useful information on selecting a journal, which you can use with any information you've learned from your rejection. Pat Thomson and Barbara Kamler's *Writing for Peer Reviewed Journals* (2013, Routledge) covers a range of issues that may have led to rejection. Wendy Belcher's *Write Your Journal Article in 12 Weeks* (2nd edition, 2019, University of Chicago Press) may also prove a useful guide. Use any reviewer comments you receive to add specificity to their advice.

When considering whether the rejection is primarily related to fit or quality, it is wise to consider how flexible those creating and maintaining the boundaries of this particular conversation are. Pat Thomson offers some useful tips (especially for early-career scholars) for identifying this issue and dealing with rejections from highly territorial journals in "When peer review is scent marking" (June 19, 2017, *Patter*, patthomson.net/2017/06/19/when-peer-review-is-scent-marking/).

Giving Feedback Constructively as a Reviewer

See notes to the previous chapter regarding the use of "gremlins" and for further reading on vulnerability and mindset.

COPE (the Committee on Publication Ethics) is a good source of advice on the ethics of publication. Their resources include some on conflict of interest (publicationethics.org/competinginterests).

As I was finalizing this *Short Guide*, I came across a comic from *The Oatmeal* (theoatmeal.com/comics/believe) about how we react emotionally to statements that (seem to) contradict firmly held beliefs. It is based on scientific research and has references (the scientific article is J.T. Kaplan, S.I. Gimbal, and S. Harris, 2016, "Neural correlates of maintaining one's political beliefs in the face of counterevidence", *Scientific Reports*, No. 6, www.nature.com/articles/srep39589).

The alignment exercise described by Havi Brooks in "Awkward conversations (and a wacky exercise)" (November 10, 2008, *Fluent Self*, www.fluentself.com/blog/habits/awkward-conversations-wacky-exercise/) may be useful for getting yourself in the right frame of mind for writing constructive feedback, especially if you feel like this manuscript needs a lot of work.

I have written more about juggling your myriad responsibilities on my website. "Juggling 101: Elements of a good plan" is a good starting point: jovanevery.ca/elements-good-plan/.

The Thomas Ricks article suggested in the notes to "What is peer review?", may help clarify the comparison between your role and that of an editor or agent for trade-published authors.

My approach to giving feedback constructively has been strongly influenced by Liz Lerman's *Critical Response Process* (2003, Liz Lerman Dance Exchange), recommended to me by an actor friend. Although designed for artists seeking in-person critique, the principles outlined in her book are valuable for academics engaging with feedback in a range of forms. Lerman's work has been especially influential in three ways: the insistence that this is the author's work and the author retains control over it; the importance of identifying what the reader has understood the text to be doing; and the importance of identifying the problem the reviewers' suggestions are addressing. Further information about her process can be found on her website, LizLerman.com/Critical-Response-Process. She has also published a book, which is available as a Kindle edition.

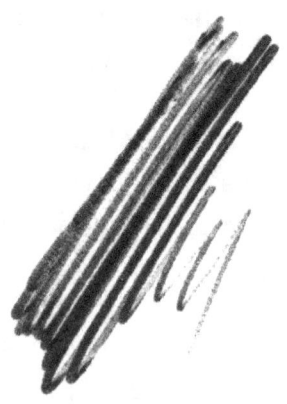

Acknowledgements

The ideas presented in this *Short Guide* have been developed over time as I have worked with academics as a coach and through the Academic Writing Studio. They have also benefited from observing the questions and frustrations academics share on Twitter, and from conversations there with those who research academic writing, those who share advice on academic writing, and with journal editors who share their experiences. Jill Anderson gave feedback on "Receiving comments as an author" when she received a revise-and-resubmit decision. Beta-readers Jennifer Andrews, Paula Barata, Rachel Bryant Davis, Jeanette Hannaford, and Bron Harrison provided helpful comments on the full draft.

As with the other books in this series, the ideas presented here were often first published on JoVanEvery.ca and have been edited and developed in this book. My first attempt to apply Liz Lerman's Critical Response Process framework in this area was in an online class, "Dealing with Reviewer Comments", several years ago. Thank you to those who participated and gave me feedback on the usefulness of that approach.

My partner, Matthew Paterson, has been willing to discuss these ideas with me as I work them out. He brings his own experience as author, reviewer, and journal editor to those conversations, and keeps me abreast of some of the practical developments. The position I take in this *Short Guide* is my own. He also provides more practical household support, including doing most of the cooking and food shopping, the importance of which cannot be overstated.

I highly recommend working with an editor. Hannah Austin edited the manuscript. Amy Crook designed the cover and the interior of the print edition. Thank you to the Alliance of Independent Authors for the wealth of practical advice they provide on self-publishing. I take full responsibility for all the decisions I have made based on the excellent advice of these professionals.

About the Author

Jo VanEvery transforms academic lives from surviving to thriving. She used to be an academic sociologist and then a programme officer for a funding agency. Now she helps you juggle your myriad responsibilities, provides a structure so you can get more writing done, helps you clarify your vision and make a plan for the next part of the path towards it, and boosts your confidence so you can do the work that makes your heart sing. You can read more of her writing on her website, JoVanEvery.ca; follow her on Twitter, Twitter.com/JoVanEvery; or like her Facebook page, Facebook.com/JoVEAcademicCareerCoach/.

Also by Jo VanEvery

Scholarly Publishing: A Short Guide (2019)
ISBN 978-1-912040-68-1 (pb) 978-1-912040-67-4 (eBook)

Finding Time For Your Scholarly Writing: A Short Guide (2018)
ISBN 978-1-912040-70-4 (pb) 978-1-912040-69-8 (eBook)

The Principles of Juggling: A Picture Book for Academics (2017)
ISBN 978-1-912040-71-1 (pb)

The Scholarly Writing Process: A Short Guide (2016)
ISBN 978-1-912040-64-3 (pb) 978-1-912040-72-8 (eBook)

Future Short Guides

I am currently rethinking how publishing this series fits with my other services. I have several more *Short Guides* in various stages of preparation, on topics including saying "no" and optimizing focus. To hear about new publications in the series, receive excerpts, and hear about work in progress, subscribe to my newsletter: JoVanEvery.ca/newsletters/

www.ingramcontent.com/pod-product-compliance
Lightning Source LLC
Chambersburg PA
CBHW071316080526
44587CB00018B/3251